(signed)

For the Library
        from ALRowse
Best Wishes .

By A.L. Rowse

A Life: Collected Poems

Transatlantic: Later Poems

SELECTED
POEMS
A.L. ROWSE

ALISON HODGE

First published in 1990 by Alison Hodge,
Bosulval, Newmill, Penzance, Cornwall TR20 8XA

British Library Cataloguing in Publication Data
Rowse, A.L. (Alfred Leslie), 1903 —
    Selected poems.
    I. Title
    821.912
    ISBN 0-906720-22-2

Designed and originated in-house.
Set in ITC Garamond.
Printed in Great Britain by BPCC Wheatons Ltd, Exeter.

Preface

I have been encouraged to make a selection of my poems by American friends, and gladly respond to the encouragement. The result is that, though I meant to make this selection representative, I may have overweighted the American section and under-represented the others. In the course of an unexpectedly long life (compensation for much illness earlier) I have written more poems that have Cornwall as background than any other. I began writing verse, and was even published, as a schoolboy, long before I dared to enter upon the arduous career of historical research and writing. In this way I have never lost touch with my roots – a dangerous thing for a poet (witness Auden) – in spite of some divagations, other scenes and temptations.

A great divagation was politics in the desperate Thirties, though a more practical involvement than other poets of that generation, not much of whose politically motivated verse has lasted. I have left hardly anything here to represent that bitter time, but more from the war to which it inevitably led.

Three backgrounds have provided inspiration for most of my verse: Cornwall, Oxford, America. Since the last appears more strongly here, I can at least plead that hardly any English poets have responded to American landscapes, scenes, experiences. A larger selection of Cornish poems might seem more appropriate for me.

The post-war period has not been a propitious time for poetry in England, any more than for other arts in such a society. Only today are people becoming aware of the vast amount of the bogus imposed upon them in 'modernist' architecture and painting.

A revolt is at last taking place in regard to those. Oddly enough it has not yet spread to the realm of poetry, though good contemporary poets, like Betjeman and Larkin, had no liking for what is imposed by the media upon the public as poetry. Nor did Eliot much care for post-Eliot verse. In fact he constantly urged that authentic poetry rested on tradition, though it does not rest there: it provides the education, the ground from which to explore further.

A.L. Rowse

Trenarren, St Austell
1990

Contents

How Many Miles to Mylor?

How many miles to Mylor
　By frost and candle-light:
How long before I arrive there,
　This mild December night?

As I mounted the hill to Mylor
　Through the dark woods of Carclew,
A clock struck the three-quarters,
　And suddenly a cock crew.

At the cross-roads on the hill-top
　The snow lay on the ground,
In the quick air and the stillness,
　No movement and no sound.

'How is it?' said a voice from the bushes
　Beneath the rowan-tree;
'Who is it?' my mouth re-echoed,
　My heart went out of me.

I cannot tell what strangeness
　There lay around Carclew:
Nor whatever stirred in the hedges
　When an owl replied 'Who-whoo?'

A lamp in a lone cottage,
　A face in a window-frame,
Above the snow a wicket:
　A house without a name.

How many miles to Mylor
　This dark December night:
And shall I ever arrive there
　By frost or candle-light?

Roseland* Year: A Children's Calendar

Come to Lamorran woods
When the snowdrops are all out,
And the February birds
With gladness begin to shout:

For the winter is now over
In the valleys of the Fal,
And Spring comes very early
By Grogoth and Tresawle.

In March or early April
Go down the banks of Gare
When the primroses are there,
And sniff the earthy air.

In sequestered lanes of Ruan
In May or late springtime
Bluebells crowd together
And ring their gallant chime.

Honeysuckle, foxgloves
Set the summer scene
All around Tresillian,
Trencreek, Goviley vean.

The Council men in autumn
Cut back the summer growth:
The ferns put forth fresh shoots
In the hedges by Trelowth.

Brown is October bracken
Where the squirrels revel
In hips and haws, the nuts
And mast of St Michael Penkevil.

About the church at Creed
Not a bud does peep:
The roses have lost their leaves
And sleep their winter sleep.

And all around the parish
The ways are white and weird:
Frost and rime on boughs
Hung with Old Man's Beard.

* Roseland means promontory land, between the Fal and the sea.

Gear

A queer place is Gear
  upon the downs
and very near to Fear
when the sun goes down
  behind the dunes,
and then you come upon
  the bare and stony places
where little skulls of animals become
  bleached and whitened bones
  that once were faces
of things that were alive like you:
the shells of snails and tiny skeletons
clean and fine, and delicate of line.
The sound of surf runs
  in your ears with the tread
  of the drowned and dead.
Here among the stones
  no one would hear the cries
  of a creature that dies.
Now the clouds rise
  no bigger than a man's finger
  to threaten the lone figure,
  spread over the land
  on either hand
  and fill the skies.
No one would hear your cries
  if you cried aloud
  to earth and cloud
No one would hear
  at Gear.

Ardevora Veor

At turn of tide, clear sky
Seventh September morn,
A boy goes sculling by
Down river from Ruan Lanihorne.

The secret flats of the Fal
Reveal unnumbered birds
Mirrored in quiet waters:
A world still beyond words.

Behind a screen of elms
A deserted house is there,
Haunted by its echo –
Ardevora, Ardevora veor.*

A herring-bone hedge of stone,
A lodge at the entrance gate,
An orchard of unpicked apples:
For whom, or what, does it wait?

Evidences of former love
And care on every side,
The anchorage, the quay:
No one comes now at the turning of the tide.

A planted berberis sheds
Its berries on the ground;
From the windlass and the well
No movement ever, and no sound.

The pretty panes are broken,
Blackberries ripen on the wall:
Peer in through the windows,
Whence no one looks out at all.

No one looks out any longer
Across the creek to the farm;
From candle-lit doorway to attic
No signal of joy or alarm.

Nor any motion of footfall
Beneath ceiling or rafter by day;
All laughter, all merriment over,
The ghosts have their way.

A house alone with its shadows,
The floors strewn with sharp glass,
What may have happened here
At Ardevora, Ardevora veor,
What estrangement come to pass?

Only an echo replies
Into the listening morn
As the solitary sculler
Moves silently down river
With the tide from Ruan Lanihorne.

* Cornish for 'the great water'.

The Old Cemetery at St Austell

Cypresses, oaks, ilexes and yews
Compose the sober scene with sombre hues;
The narrow path runs down the southward slope
Among the graves, where our forefathers sleep
In the sure and certain hope of resurrection:
Head to foot they lie, looking to the east

Whence cometh their salvation – or so at least
They thought in former, simpler days. No such
Certainty now: all we know is that they
Are asleep hard by where they lived their useful lives;
Here they still are together, husbands and wives,
Fathers and children: in death they are not lost.

They lie in the heart of the parish, edge of the town,
On the hillside that looks to the sun going down:
On the skyline the ruined engine-house
Of Polgooth Mine, whence the town took its rise
From whose rich veins and from whose merchandise
The generations of vanished miners fed.

I see them: so many insects on the heave of hill
Scurrying about, burrowing underground;
If you listen closely you may hear the sound
Of the rumour of their toil, the dead men sing
Along their levels and hidden galleries,
A remote murmur like a hive of bees.

Yet not so: they are all fled over the seven seas:
Ruin descended on the mines and these
Men were driven forth to earn their bread
In America, Australia, Africa.
These are our exiles: they have left their bones
In foreign soil, under other stones.

There in the distance are the dark woods of Penrice,
Mysterious, aloof, funereal;
Lost in their depths lies the house of the Admiral,
The last Sir Charles: whose family did well

In the time of the Commonwealth and showed a nice
Sense of the moment, laid out their moneys with skill,

Adding acre to acre and field to field.
The squawk of pheasants now for generations
Has announced the vicinity of the squire. Yet still
Their tribute to mortality they yield,
Having come to an end with a young heir killed
In Nineteen Fourteen, in that war of nations.

For him the white gate on the road to Trenarren
Stands open in vain, in vain the long curve of the drive
Leads across deerpark and ploughland in the wavering
Moonlight, to the wide portico welcoming
The returned, the family portraits in the hall:
He has become but a tablet on a wall.

The little chantry chapel in the church
Is filled with their memorials. Here as a boy
I used to sit in the darkling evening
Deep-ensconced in a pew, listening
To the organ's music, rapt with such extreme
Joy, my mind enchanted moved in a dream,

In which were mingled melodies and urns,
A woman weeping over a bier, coloured
Armorial bearings, glints of crimson and gold,
White marble stained with the late westering sun's
Last gleams. Heaven itself seemed to unfold
In those rich harmonies the echoing rolled

Like waves within the caverns on the coast,
And caught me up upon their crest, until
The painted roof inlaid with golden stars
Rolled back, and there revealed a miracle:
God on His throne, the Son and Holy Ghost,
Amid the beating wings of the angel host.

Where now is the stone put up to commemorate
Those four young men drowned while crossing the bay

One day in the seventies? I used to meditate
Much on them and wonder at their fate:
What sudden squall of wind capsized their boat
That September afternoon and swept them away?

Twenty and twenty-one, twenty-seven and eighteen
They were – their names no one remembers now –
Many times I have thought of them and seen
Their little craft fighting her way through the waves,
Till rounding the point or farther out in the bay
She disappears and they are lost to their loves,

Who should have been fathers of families:
Yet now they are forever young. Not here
Under the friendly turf, the shade of the trees
Will you find them, but out there, the whitened skulls
Washed by the tides, wedged in the crevices
Of the rocks, mouthed by fishes, eyed by the gulls.

Who are all these? Here one who lost a foot
At Inkerman and returned to keep a mill
At Tregonissey; yet another fought
In Afghanistan; a few were mariners,
But most of them were farmers, labourers
In the fields, ploughmen, small traders, carpenters.

Now their account books are all closed up:
It has ceased to matter whether they were happy
More than a century ago, or whether
In their long absence some one else slept
With their wives, or if their children were another's:
What do these things matter in the eye of death?

I note the names: Treleaven and Rosevear,
Hobba and Jago, Hocking, Rowse and Faull,
Veale and Dunn and Drew, Trudgian and Penhall,
Sampson Borlase and his Rebecca, and here
A stranger to the parish, Abraham Dear.
Across his name the vivid ivies scrawl.

Amid so much human mutability
This walled garden is a place of rest and peace:
Death loses its horrid aspect, is seen to be
A natural term to life's unquietness:
Here all conflict is stilled, quarrels cease,
Here is neither friend nor enemy.

Yet most of them knew each other at market
And feast and fair; and some kept company
Before marrying another with whom they lie.
Here are two lovers who fell from the quay
One December night in eighteen thirty three,
And were drowned. Remember them, of your charity.

It is a Sunday morning in war-time. The bells
Are silent though it is church-time, and they
Ring out and up the hillside usually
To this garden, summoning the dead company
To worship with the living. A thrush on a grey
Headstone halts to eye me inquisitively,

Then flits away. On the road outside resound
The footsteps of people passing by to church:
You see the old superstition still has its pull
Among the old-fashioned and respectable;
If you wait, you will see the little organist
Go bustling by like a bird that hops on the ground.

The sun is on the eastern face of the tower;
Through a break in the trees you see the clock: the hour
Is close on eleven. A scented summer breeze
Lifts and lets fall again the fronds of the trees;
The grass is strewn with flowers of ilexes
And early leaves, the rhododendrons blown.

What is this secret scent upon the air
So subtle it steals in everywhere? It is
The odour of resin in the cypresses

And yews, rising in the heat, a honeyed breath.
In his remote still corner a snake lies sleeping,
Emblem of wisdom, of knowledge after death.

The hours go by and now it is afternoon:
The white sail of a gull crosses the blue
Peacock sky that remembers Italy:
The sun goes round to the western face of the tower,
The majestic image of the Trinity,
The Virgin, the Angel of the Annunciation, the Flower.

There too is the holy hermit, St Austell, from whom
The parish derives its name, who lived by his well
Preaching, performed an occasional miracle.
O holy, blessed and glorious Trinity,
Three Persons and One God, One in Three:
How comparatively simple all would be

If this indeed were all. My mind returns
To the Feast-days, Trinity Sundays, of the past:
The church all breathing flowers, the white linens
Upon the altar, the stiff new surplices,
The festal air, the silver chalices,
The procession, the vague old vicar wandering, lost:

Then home through the hot, sweet-smelling summer lanes,
Gay with the first foxgloves and purple vetches,
Red sorrel and golden crowsfoot in the hedges,
To Sunday dinner, family round the table
Together, who now are all scattered, east and west,
And one has gone to his eternal rest.

The poets, my friends, have written learnedly
On Time Present, Time Past and Time to come,
But I do not know that they have added to the sum
Of what we knew before, and that is simply:
All creatures come by their appointed end;
Let us learn to look on death, then, as a friend.

Hark! from a field comes the comfortable sound
Of a reaper near-by harvesting his hay –
Even as these in their day were harvested.
There is speedwell growing here on the little mound
Of a child; a tiny lizard comes out to look
At the man who is strangely moved as he reads in his book:

'I am the Resurrection and the Life.'
So many times have these poor simple folk
Heard and taken comfort, since they must,
In these magnificent words. 'And when this mortal
Shall put on immortality': the recital
Tells nothing: we only know that dust is dust.

Yet that indeed is not all: they scattered their seed,
Before they died, like flowers upon the air.
They are our forefathers, from whom we were begotten:
Their blood runs in my veins. Therefore have I come
To fulfil my childhood's pledge and fashion this prayer.
In the place that knew them they shall not be forgotten.

1937

Behold the antics of the populace:
Here in a corner in a close embrace

A loving couple without shape or grace
Front to front, vapid face to face.

A toddling father with his toddling child
Walks in the meadows in the warm and mild

Weather, has no thoughts to occupy
His vacant mind, nothing to signify

Except the daily round by tube and train
And bus, from home to town and back again;

His constant one concern to earn enough
To keep his woman and his child, a roof

Over their heads and the garage: pity
Him. Behold the fresh youth of the city

Enter now the walks with unseeing eyes,
Loud of mouth, whose voices hold no surprise.

A day will come when there shall descend on them
From the skies they do not observe, some stratagem

Of fate to search and sear their flesh with fire,
Seal the eyes that are stupid with desire:

Liquid fire will rain down from the air,
Will suddenly arrive upon them there

And lick their bodies up and burn their bones,
No-one at hand to hear their mutual groans:

For these are they who, warned of what's to come,
Walk blindly on to their appointed doom.

Trenarren: 1941

The thunder-green sea
Brings nearer the Island
On which stood the chapel
Of Michael the Archangel.

Smoke from a chimney
In the V-shaped valley,
The voices of children,
A robin on the bough:

Familiar and cheerful
Domestic noises
Speak of contentment
About me now.

But what is to come?
I ask myself, waiting
In this burial-place
Of my ancient people:

The long-headed, dark-faced
Mediterranean
Men who drove prows
Into these inlets:

Confronting the danger
That they too awaited
In the urgent whisper,
The winter sea waiting.

Duporth Hill

The moon lies white upon the corn,
  The noisy trees are all still;
Silent are the footsteps now
  That used to ring on Duporth Hill.

Where are the Worcesters, the Gloucester lads,
  The Cornwalls and the Somersets,
Who kept their watch upon these coasts
  Where glows the light of late sunsets?

They stood on guard that bitter year
  Of our defeat, by night and day;
Over the hill the bugles sounded;
  A day came and they marched away.

The sky-line rises to the west
  A mounded form, a darker frieze;
Shades of former figures weave
  In and out the moon-blanched trees.

Where are they now who once were here?
  In Egypt, Libya, Palestine,
Scattered across the seven seas,
  Where long alone they held their line

Nor ever surrendered to despair.
  Others there are who now are still:
Silent are the eager steps
  That used to ring on Duporth Hill.

As I Go Down Trenarren Lane

As I go down Trenarren Lane
  Stonecrop and scabious star the hedges;
A yellow-hammer sings on a bough,
  Rest-harrow, thyme and purple vetches.

'A little bit of bread and no cheese'
  Says the yellow-hammer on the bough;
Birds and flowers, a solitary heart
  The company the place has now.

In Memory: Adam von Trott

The raging sun-struck sea explodes
In beauty round the rocks.
Who could have known when I knew you first
Of such a fate in store for you,
Laid upon that grave and lovely head?
I look up at the house you knew,
Grey among the stripped autumnal trees;
Down upon the shore
The spring-tide flows up to the purple cliffs.
The spring-tide of your life already over,
I meditate upon it here alone,
Unsure what part I had in your strange fate.
The white horses march across the bay,
The targets bob up and down like buoys.
There is Duporth, here the sacrificial grove,
Here on the headland I saw the Ship of Death.
Now you over the sea,
The hangman's noose about your neck,
Sleep soundly in a traitor's grave.

Corpus Garden

Maytime's come in Corpus garden
As in a green, leaf-shadowed room,
With wallflowers and forget-me-nots,
Auriculas and golden broom.

The young men who've returned from war
Play at bowls in the level sun:
The dull woods, knocking against each other,
Resound. And now the play is done.

A canon's ducks quack over the wall,
Echo their reverend owner's words;
Blood-red peonies light the border,
And all the trees are alive with birds.

A little wind now lifts the leaves
And whispering lets them fall again;
A lyric thrush pours out his song;
Columbines, lupins just begin.

Turning round I see your window
Wide-open, cool and summery;
Beneath the sill wistaria droops,
Hanging like vines of Italy.

The window opens a dead mouth
Into the darkness of a tomb:
How well I knew in former years
Its green and friendly summer gloom.

Maytime's come in Corpus garden –
But you have not survived your war,
Who lie with Shelley and Trelawny
Under a cold indifferent star.

Alfoxden

Along the roads of Somerset
　We walk, my friend and I,
To Alfoxden from Nether Stowey
　Beneath the April sky.

The hedges starred with primroses,
　The woods with hollies gleam,
The world wakes out of winter sleep —
　Yet we move in a dream.

Two other friends there are that walk
　Out of an earlier time,
Who often came this way together
　And heard the self-same chime

From all the birds that haunt the coverts
　And all the woodland rides.
Noon strikes across the quiet field
　The shadowed tower bestrides.

By Holford church we leave the roads
　And make into the hills;
And now a sound most musical
　The listening forest fills:

The sound of running water, cool
　As a thousand freshet springs
That run together in a secret glade
　Where all the woodland sings.

And here is the sacred river Alph
　That, in the poem, ran
Down to the sunless sea, through caverns
　Measureless to man.

Now the house breaks on the view
　In the curve of the quiet hills,
The silver beeches of the park,
　A pool of daffodils.

Deep in the brake above the house,
  Under an oak we lie,
All through the dreaming afternoon
  Beneath the blue coned sky.

Silence: no movement and no sound:
  Nor yet a leaf that stirs:
Only the birds that come and go,
  Those singing voyagers.

The sun gleams white upon the front
  Of that enchanted place
Looking upwards to the hills,
  The haunts of ancient peace.

Everything is hushed and still:
  Some magic of the sea
Has fallen on roof and ledge and sill,
  On every twig and tree.

But whose are those figures that emerge
  And cross the printed lawn,
One with slow step and sure, the other
  Shy as a startled fawn?

Though all is still, he hears the woods
  Raging like the sea;
He hears the voices of things growing
  Calling him silently.

He studies the path of the crescent moon,
  Though the sun is high and bright,
And watches the eyes of the fallow deer
  Shine in the white moonlight;

Walks once more in the shadowy groves
  In the cool of the slow day's end,
After long parting and separation
  Meets once more with his friend.

The presence of genius is over all
  And such its inner power
That time stands still beneath its spell:
  Once more it is their hour ...

The hours go by, and we return
  Along the woodland ways
From Alfoxden to Nether Stowey
  In the afternoon heat-haze.

The singing woods of Aldfoxden
  Behind us in the lee,
We leave the hills – the plain ahead –
  And in the west, the sea.

The Choice

O look at all the apple blossom, the buds of May
That dress with white and glimmering array
The lawns of Spring at the mid-moment of evening;
O look at the lemon-green of lime, gold beech, dark yew,
The plumes of poplar waving together to the east;
All the trees in the garden are singing in the silence.
O Life, O World, O Time, if only to arrest this moment! –
But time moves on into a world that knows one not.

Look now upon this other side:
The formal magnificence, the Roman world of stone,
The wheeling dome with its volutes and urns,
This learned prison, the walls that shut me in,
This shuttered quarry, the coldness of the tomb,
This cemetery with its monuments.

Like a madman I go from one side to the other,
Look out upon this scene and now on that,
Avid of life, by fever of mind possessed,
Poised like the frozen eagle for flight into the unknown,
Confront the formal West, turned like him to stone.

January Fire

The girl is gone:
Along the pavement I watch her walk alone,
Self-possessed and elegant and sad:
No-one to escort her through the street
To her supposititious destination,
That is but a station on the way,
But another beginning
To a journey that has no end:
Having found the promise of another spring
But another deception
In the game that offers no solution,
The play that has no answer to the question,
The dance no end.
Behind the dark and leaning dome
The sky is aflame with January fire:
The universe opens its heart,
The Arctic pathways of the unattainable,
Transitory glory of the untrodden rose
That illuminates the pathos of our state,
The sunset caught in the candid eye
Of the girl now turning the corner of the street:
To whom I have said goodbye.

I look out on the wounded world,
For a moment hesitate
Before drawing the sombre curtains over
The disturbing splendour and the glow
In the west, return to learned order and the gloom
Of the disciplined, deserted room.

Lazarus in New College Chapel

This is Lazarus: the head an egg
Laid upon labouring shoulders,
Or like a stone laid upon a cave.
The clear spring light gives life
Making the cold stone breathe and move.
Awake, O awake from the dream of death,
After four days laid in the grave,
The mumbled lips still shut, breath
Withheld, tongue seeking an outlet,
The eyes still sealed in sleep
Resisting awakening, the pain and grief
Of life, the body unfree, still bound
In the wound grave-clothes,
Arms pinioned, arrested in motion,
The body's life stirring in the wrapped
Limbs, now lapped and lipped in light
Passing a bird's wing over the stone erect.
Now a cloud sends Lazarus back to the dead;
And now the returning sun
Of spring, of moving wings and flowers
Shooting from the earth-bound soil,
Of birds calling in the grove,
Calls him to awake and live.

This is Lazarus: this is he
Whom Jesus loved, over whom
He wept when they had laid him in the tomb
On the bitter road out of Bethany.
Now he has heard the word: see
The coffined breast bursting the bonds,
Leaning forward, urgent for life.
Not the life of stone intolerable to be borne
But the life of moving things,
Of growing flowers and birds' wings.
In the stillness of the cave,
In the still chapel of the grave North
He begins to stir and move:
He has heard the Word:
'Lazarus, come forth!'

Kierkegaard: Copenhagen

His life was a perpetual Lutheran Sunday,
Cheerless, loveless, impotent and null,
Tortured alike by doubt and doubting faith,
Lacerated by the sense of sin,
The guilt brought down upon his innocent head
By the father who, driven by a rebellious will,
From a hill in Jutland cursed God and all his works.

Now he sits in the cold autumnal garden
Melancholy with the weight of the curse
Upon him, the sin of the father visited
On him, the cheerful sparrows at his feet
Unseeing, the ducks of the world of Hans Andersen –
A family party on the pond – unheeding,
Nor feels upon the weary leaden shoulders
The soft caress of birch fronds as they wave
To and fro, moving in the autumn wind,
Lightly touch and withdraw – a woman's hair.

This is the latitude of Edinburgh,
The latitude of the tortured conscience,
I remember. In this kingdom he received
The stigmata of genius and pain,
Imprisoned in the primal fear of the flesh,
As now in lead and stone.

                    I am back again
In the garden – the clock strikes the three quarters –
My footsteps lead me to seek the company
Of the solitary man whose mind researched
Into the innermost recesses of guilt
As the tongue seeks the sore place in the tooth.
Inventor of the formula of *Angst*,
Come and solace me now, you who knew
The strength in the treacherous reserves of doubt,
The courage and contempt to be found in fear,
The consolations and solitariness.
Your eyes that now see nothing once looked out
On human misery and understood

Every inflection of its voice and mood,
Hugged its satisfactions to yourself,
The concave mirror of a fractured world,
Where all is microscopically clear:
The nightmare of a too percipient mind.

Aloft he sits, slightly askew on his chair,
Uneasily to the world, alone and very famous,
The man who died of spiritual pride.

T. E. Lawrence

Whitsun pours out from the churches on to the pavement
And in the petals pattering under the rain;
Impoverished ladies in Edwardian hats
Shuffle along in their penurious goloshes.
The naughty choirboys leapfrog out of church.
This is the Betjeman country –
Laburnum, copper-beech and may –
On my way past St Philip and St James
Along the roaring Woodstock Road to quiet Polstead.
The sanctus-bell of St Margaret's rings
For the Elevation unheeded by the former occupants.
But they are all gone away, they are shadows now,
And I wait in vain under the rain,
Under the flowering may, for one or other to appear.
Within, the windows are the same, the outlook
On the acacias opposite, the red chestnut
Over the wall that lit up with summer dawns,
For ever beckoning to the East, grown bigger now.
By the path a rambler rose, peonies and arabis,
A white flowering shrub beside the Gothic porch,
Planted by father, flowers bravely still.

Whitsun morning and no-one appears,
No-one who knows what in former years
Went on there, or what moves the stranger to tears –
The five boys bent on bikes, mad on architecture –
Nor what brought the mother and father
So strangely to rest together here.
A motor-bicycle comes up the road
Too swiftly, disturbs the dream
With sudden approximation to reality.

This is how the boy whose genius brings all alive
Came to his expected end,
By then, choosing death rather for his friend.
'These journeys, you know, don't really end
Till we do.' And again, 'The difficulty
Is to keep oneself untouched in a crowd,
In a populous place find solitude.'

'It were well if from the universe
All animal creation had been left out.'
How can he have come to this,
The glad and eager boy, living his life
In the boy's world of fantasy and innocence?
Writing home to mother from the dark womb
Of St Sauveur at Caen, now all ruin and desolation,
The punctuated end of a civilisation.
When did he learn, the boy who found out
That life was an enacted lie,
No faith holds, no bond or love or loyalty,
And laid aside the name to which he had brought fame,
Renouncing friends, with whom he had once felt,
Renouncing art, skill of brain and government,
Renouncing life itself,
To breathe out his spirit on a road's green verge.
Some trauma of the soul, some wound
Beneath the skull, some revelation
Of the fact of life that stopped the flow
And shattered the cherished fantasy,
The world of innocence for ever gone.

Jumbo Jet

In this plane I'm just a parcel.
No longer an individual soul;
The minute of tension, the moment of take-off
Is over, and all is yet in control.

In this jumbo jet of latest design
Three hundred such human parcels are we;
Flight is westward along with the sun,
The plane crowded to capacity.

But suppose if the plane loses height,
In course of landing goes out of control:
Will each of the three hundred parcels
Rate an individual soul?

Abraham Lincoln at Springfield

The house at the corner of Eighth and Jackson Streets
Now buff-painted, green-shuttered as of old –
The brass plate gives you the name of the occupant
That was: *Abraham Lincoln.* Enter now.
Within, the wine-coloured light of October falls,
Filtered through Victorian curtains looped and fringed,
On figured carpet and mahogany furniture,
Falls on the horse-hair sofa of extra length
To accommodate the long lean figure of a man
Of melancholy aspect, marked by fate
In the sad depths of the eyes, the lines of the face,
The full foreknowledge of man's tragedy
The burden upon him, a willing sacrifice.
Afternoon light spills into the sitting room
All honey and gold, has nothing of crimson in it:
All is placid and calm. Turn but the corner,
And here the family is together once more,
Mary Todd coming downstairs from her room,
To see to things for Robert's coming home,
The sullen difficult son at odds with father.
The still, reflective house wakes from its trance
For an evening-party for the legislator-elect:
Lights in the chandeliers, Mrs Lincoln in silk
And lace fichu receives the visitors,
Friends and neighbours, folks with full arms,
Bringing good wishes for Thanksgiving Day.

Here are the fragments of family life shored up
Against a day of ruin – Thad's little chair,
Favourite companion of the President –
Who died in the White House at the worst of the war,
Leaving the sad heart lonelier still.
See here on a bracket the logman's scrawny hand
That signed the Emancipation of the slaves.
A long shadow falls athwart the room
Obscuring the latticed sun, leaving an outline
Hard to glimpse amid the dancing motes
That register life in all created things:
The shadow is of the dead, that speaks a tongue

More moving to the imagination than what's alive.
Observe the sprawling figure on the floor
Playing with the cat, a fondness he had
Improbably in common with Richelieu,
Some solace for the politic cast of mind.

The day comes to take leave of this loved house.
Loved? – yet always the sense of insatisfaction,
Desire unfulfilled and disenchanted love –
Folks crowding round for an affectionate farewell,
To hear the familiar voice for the last time:
'My Friends, No-one not in my situation
Can appreciate my feeling of sadness at this
Parting. To this place and the kindness of these
People I owe everything. Here
I have lived a quarter of a century,
And have passed from a young man to an old man.
Here my children have been born, and one is buried.
I now leave, not knowing when or whether
Ever I may return, with a task before me
Greater than that which rested upon Washington.'*
(He dreams again of the ship with black sails,
Forewarning of what, omen that never fails.)

Too late, at last the son comes to revere
The famous father he had not loved in life,
Himself an old man now in Washington
Would every evening have his carriage driven
To look on the lighted figure, his father's shrine
Where now aloft, the slain god of the Republic
Sits with open welcoming arms to the throng,
The moving escalator of citizens,
Of sailors and airmen, fathers handing their children
Up the high steps where now he belongs to the ages.

* These are the words of his Farewell Speech.

The Stranger at Gettysburg

Here is Seminary Ridge where they stood
Those first July days of 1863:
Below the Ridge the Lutheran Seminary
With round cupola from which the generals,
First Union, then Confederate, surveyed the scene.
They used the dormitory as a hospital.
Now it's early spring, and the mocking-bird
Calls chuck-chuck-chuck, sweet-sweet.
Within, the clear sun of Pennsylvania
Comes silvered through chapel windows:
Ein feste Burg ist unser Gott.

Powhattan Artillery and Dance's Battalion
Reached the field at evening to turn their batteries
On Cemetery Hill: the great cannonade
Before Longstreet's assault on the Ridge.
Pickett's Division of Longstreet's Corps,
Marching from Chambersburg, arrived after sunset;
Stuart's Cavalry from Hanover engaged Hampton's
In the summer evening at Hunterstown.
In Shultz Woods guns blazed among rocks and oaks;
Troops concentrating at the end of June,
Converging upon this murderous moment of time.

In the early morning, soldiers bivouacked,
Smoke of breakfast rising among trees;
Lee, thoughtful and calm on 'Traveller':
'If ours were not so bloody a business,
What a wonderful spectacle!'

Line of battle formed on either side the pike,
The McMillan house, high on the ridge, saw all.
Thomas's brigade of Georgia Infantry
Moved across the pike into McMillan Woods.
Crows fly these peopled solitudes,
Glisten funereal on Cemetery sky-line,
Where now dead cannon balls gleam and shine.

To the west, then in setting sun –
The slopes of South Mountain, now shorn and bare;
Squirrels frolic among the falling shadows.
Here stood North Carolina under command,
Brockenborough, Heth and Pettigrew,
Her regiments in action all through
Those days – one Confederate soldier
In four who fell was a North Carolinian.
All these are English names. A sentinel bird
Is surprised at the stranger in tears
At these men's memorial.

The opposing ridge is a graveyard of monuments –
Two carrion crows fight the battle over again
Across the intervening space. Still
The North Carolina colour-bearer thrusts
His flag forward against a burst of copse;
Still the bugler-boy sounds the assault
For Virginia – looks across to where
The Pennsylvania Centre holds fast.

Oak leaves of winter scatter like paper
Where then the foliage was full on the trees.
Stillness, sun and quiet where so many died.
Big Round Top and Little Round Top
Close the view in the morning haze.
Suddenly a jay rends the silence
With the scream of a wounded man.

The breeze brings balm as there was none
In those hot days of '63, under the sun.
Here the Georgia Infantry broke the Union line
At the Angle – attacked in flank, the Federals
Fought their way out with heavy loss.
A pheasant squawks a comment upon
The Army of Northern Virginia
        against the Army of the Potomac.

From little Round Top one sees the mountains,
The whole Confederate position screened by woods:
Longstreet's Corps drove back the Union line
Entrenched from Devil's Den to Peach Orchard.
Here Massachusetts held firm amid the boulders,
Where Father William Corby, chaplain of brigade,
Bearded, in long coat, stole over shoulders,
Gave absolution to all men on the field,
Killing each other.
New York Engineers bivouacked by
Hummelbaugh House, bullet holes in the barn,
Where hyacinths now bloom,
The catkins coming out on Culp's Hill;
In the creek the early peepers
Keep up their perpetual whirr.
From Jeb Steuart's monument
A nut-hatch drops, eyes the stranger
Meditating the mingled glory
And idiocy of men.

A broad-shouldered veteran of the late war
Surveys the field with practised eye.
Behind where Maine Infantry stood
Sharp-shooters came round out of the wood.
Young saplings stand erect and straight.
A deer crops here where New York Cavalry
Were halted, eyes the stranger, puts up
A white scut of tail, vanishes into cover.
From Meade's Headquarters Old Glory flies over
Alike the blue and the grey.
Today, a robin chatters among silent guns.
At the crossroads to Hagerstown
The retreat took place, behind breast works
Thrown up along the road to Waynesborough;
And Lee withdrew.

Drifts of dead oak leaves dried in the channels,
The trees begin again to put forth leaf.
A flicker of crimson-headed woodpecker
Crosses the path of the Stranger:
Silence and sun and sadness in the air,
Spring and a hint of Resurrection,
No more.

All Souls Day in Wyoming

The saddle-back hills and cattle millionaires
Of Omaha are a November night away:
I wake to find the country white with frost,
Snow-fences already up along the track.
We're in Wyoming and, high up, shortly stop
At Laramie of the old Oregon Trail:
Beside the station a dainty yellow coach
Used in Yellowstone in earlier days.
All night we have been slowly climbing up
To this bare plateau, snow mist over uplands,
Nothing in sight but cattle and icy streams,
Nothing but the ghosts of vanished Indians,
A hawk planes over the wastes, and here and there
A house huddles beside the railroad track.
The long slow reptile of the train winds round
A bluff, piñons holding to the living rock.

This is Rock Springs, an arctic settlement
Of miners, seeking gold and drilling oil.
Green River, a platform swept by bitter wind:
I scurry to the warm station-hall and return
With *The Quiet American*. Onward we go
Through driving sleet and vagrant snow that shuts
Out all but the vicinity of railroad sidings,
Disused coaches, metal containers, huts.
Now over the Continental Divide the ground
Is free of snow: haystacks stand in meadows,
Some trees and ragged willows flushed with red;
Overhead, a flight of mallard from the lake.
At Soda Springs, a desolate hard-bitten spot
With stores for Stockmen's Hardware, Groceries,
The bars and dives that nourish their hardened lives.

As day draws in, I see a different scene:
Candles lit in a dark panelled room
Flicker in the pools of mahogany,
Firelight on coved ceiling, a bust of Wren
Looking serene on the familiar gathering;
The glasses are filled with wine, the feast wears on.

This is All Souls' Night. The great Christ Church bell
And many a lesser bell sound through the room.
Perhaps a ghost may come, for it is a ghost's right.
I eat the bread of voluntary exile:
Alone in this wilderness I celebrate.

Muskingum

'Jesus increased in wisdom and stature, and in
favour with God and Man.'
***

Away from the Presbyterian platitudes of the college
Here is a place where the chipmunks forage
Gold-striped in the grass, sit up to eye
        The suspect stranger.

Mid-morning, yet the Hallow-e'en moon
Leers high over the girls' gaunt dormitory,
Where they dream their innocent dreams to be
        Mothers of the nation.

Sycamore, maple, willow, dogwood –
A blue jay scolds the quiet neighbourhood;
The monogamous swans in conjugal amity
        Patrol the lake.

Blue asters fringe the stream below the Fall
Tapestry of verdure, russet and gold.
A sanctus bell breaks the silence to recall
        The ages of faith.

Penetrate the Hollows, where the leaves
Have lived their lives and now detach themselves
Softly from the trees, with papery sound
        Fall to the ground.

The fallen giant of primeval forest gives
The illusion of Châteaubriand's Ohio:
At the end of the sunlit glade Atala
        Perhaps may appear.

Over the rustic bridge the pretty girls pass,
Rackets in hand. The leaves strew the grass
Even as they will be strewn in their season:
        Since all things pass.

Under the Pillared Portico

Driven by the mad professor in the beaver hat
Into the campus superfluously late at night,
Up the snow-covered, ice-bound hill
Suddenly, swiftly swerving round the bend
I catch sight of a lighted scene to chill
The heart, a blow between the unwilling eyes:
Under the arclight of the pillared portico
A rite enacted on the open stage,
Oblivious of time and light and passers-by.
There in the eye of the world for all to see,
Uncaring, mute, in silent ecstasy,
Two lovers in passionate stillness: he
Tall and columnar, slender as the pillar
Erect before the sacrificial act,
Gold-crowned as the god: while she
Held in his arms in one unconscious world
With him. 'Each hath one and is one'
Might be their motto, if they had heard of Donne,
'John Donne, Undone' – by love undone;
Nor any more aware than he
What time will do to turn the trance to prison,
Reveal no world to discover
In one or other lover.
Such are the thoughts that rage
In that age of unwanted revelation
While the car wheels round
And with it the darkened city.

Portrait of a German Woman

Monumental, *unsterblich,* bloody German *Frau,*
Out of whom came the robots who ruined the world,
Hard, unsmiling face, with eyes unseeing,
Turned in upon yourself, rapt
In contemplation of what deadly dream,
What ecstasy of blood and iron, breeding
Sons for *Deutschland, Deutschland über Alles.*
Inconsiderate of ill, under your enormous hat,
Like the Kaiserin's in the Tiergarten
Now shattered in a thousand pieces:
Behind you I see Krupp, Thyssen and Stinnes,
The malign *Macht* that wrecked our century.
Woman with a stance like a Budda, but evil,
Abstracted from the beauty of the world,
The crimson flowers beside you unheeding:
Yet conscious perhaps of the fate laid on you,
Priestess carrying your unspeakable burden,
Woman of iron, with hands upon your womb,
Woman of the sorrowful face, and of the wrath to come.

President J. F. Kennedy

How like the age to lop the tallest flower,
A common age that envies quality.
On this malign day the mountains are lovely still:
The San Gabriel range looks down unknowing
Upon the fractured Mission of his faith,
Where the Fathers lived their spartan lives.
Today the scene is sadder for unfeeling beauty,
Unconcerned with the ills of man, unsharing
Our concern, our grief for loss irreparable.
The cool and golden head that held all clear
Shattered by an irrelevant lunatic shot;
The voice that spoke hope to a discordant world
Suddenly stilled, in the twinkling of an eye;
The courage that had come through waters of the Pacific
Stopped by a bullet in a chance Dallas street:
Everything in that too fortunate life –
The golden youth so carefully groomed,
So nurtured, so prepared for politics,
All fated to lead to this unmeaning moment,
This meeting with destiny, this encounter
From what different paths, of slayer and the slain.
The map of life, full of promise and smiling hope,
All spread out like a mountain slope,
Suddenly crumpled in a blood-stained car.

To what purpose? To what end?
Nothing that can portend
Any good to the human condition;
Nothing that means anything,
Or speaks anything but misery.
Let him that can then pray – for what
Consolation that offers in a faithless time,
When even crime has no face of grandeur,
Nothing in it but insignificant and mean
To bring disgrace upon the human scene.

The Forest Ranger

Sim Jarvi, the tall forest ranger,
Slim and sun-crowned Finn, died here.
By birth an Oregonian, all his life
He gave to the service of forest and mountain:
Here at Sierra Alta remember him.
He knew the secret lair of mountain lion
And where lurked the black bear: killer
And prey were alike to him, both in his care.
The lion roaring after his prey doth seek
His meat from God. To him each had his place
In the harmony of nature, less red
In tooth and claw than the great killer: man.
His clear blue eye would scan the mountain face,
Detect outlined against blue rim of sky
The big-horned sheep or shy mule-deer.
Racoons would come to him to be fed. Even
The rattler crossing his path had no hurt of him.

He knew all the trails like the veins on his hand,
All the secrets of that upheaved land lay
Open to him: the lateral fronds of white fir,
The silver bark of canyon oak, even
The sharp thorns of buckrush were his friends.
He loved the rough striations of the rocks,
Black and white like a giant panda, grey
Or burnt umber and ochre, sepia and rose.
Taking a few wafers and raisins, a flask
Of water to quench his thirst, he would quest all day
Under the sun, in and out the cool shade
Of sugar pines, or the stiff Jeffery firs,
The petrified skeletons of trees
Laid waste by lightning or by forest fire.

On such a July day, the noonday sun
Bringing out the resinous scents,
The aromatic odours of manzanita
And yucca – our Lord's candle – he lay down to die,
Alone in the loved high altitudes:
No one around, only a cicada singing,

In the silent solitudes no breath nor sound.
At night a little wind arose to play
With the fronds of his hair and cool his brow there
Where he lay – of your charity remember him –
Under the glittering Californian stars.

Christmas in California

There is the mass of mountains under the moon,
There are the lights of Arcadia, green and gold;
Here the palms and olives, Monterey pines:
How different a landscape as I grow old
From the simple and innocent slopes I knew as a child,
Up the furze-parks to the downs of Carclaze,
Past the claypits and clear pools by the road,
The scent of heather and thyme where the sheep graze:
Carn Grey on the skyline looming over the bay,
The same moon suffusing the coast with its glow
For a boy homeward-bound those years ago,
The moorland scent in nostrils as he mounted the hill
In the sharp air towards Christmas, thinking he still
Saw the star above Bethlehem, the faithful shepherds
Keeping their flocks on a similar night,
The Magi make their pilgrimage all in a row,
As if all the mystery of the Orient were there
Over the rim of the headland bathed in light,
The bay filled to the brim with gold, and not far
The Wise Men, Caspar, Melchior, Balthasar.

Death-Bed

Late September sun fills the room with light
Where my mother is lying,
Ribbons in her hair, hands shrunken on the white
Counterpane: she has gone back to childhood:
She is dying.

Through the open window in this strange house
I see in the afternoon haze St Stephen's church-tower,
Where as a boy I sang and returning late
My mother came down from the village to wait
For me in the summer night.

She is beyond remembering, she is already elsewhere,
The liquid eyes clouded, the speech thickening.
She has been waiting for me to come:
It is the hour of Evening Prayer.

'Lighten our darkness, we beseech Thee, O Lord,
And by thy great mercy defend us
From all perils and dangers of this night,
For the love of Thy only Son,
Our Saviour, Jesus Christ. Amen.'
She does not speak again.

It seems that this was what she was waiting for
To die in peace. Too delicate,
Too proud, to ask. All too late
We come together after years estranged,
And still we do not meet.

It is too late. If only one might recall
The bitter words, the anguished years:
I bury my head on her breast.
Too late, now gentle as a child at rest,
She is no longer here.

Quietly I withdraw from the light-filled room,
Taking my last look at the familiar face,
Already so strange, head fallen to one side:
I leave her in this stranger's house, I
Leave her there to die.

Passion Sunday in Charlestown Church

The rain beats down remorselessly
From beech and chestnut on the graves;
My young cousin lies beside the porch.
The parish is all gathered in the church,
The minute bell clangs, last footsteps hurry,
The Mass about to begin.
The priest in blood-red chasuble
Brings in the elements, a lighted candle
Goes before; the handsome, dark-haired thurifer
Erect, a slimmer Felix Randal,
Comes down to cense the faithful.
He bows, the parish returns his salutation,
Even the one stray sheep returned
To watch, observe, mumble with his lips,
Go through the familiar childhood ritual,
Tears hardly held back from the eyes –
Hoping it might be so – while the chants rise:
   Kyrie Eleison,
   Christe Eleison,
   Kyrie Eleison.
Rain patters on the roof,
The wind rushes in the gutters,
Attention wanders, till the Creed:
And was incarnate by the Holy Ghost,
And was made man.
The Parish falls on knees, then shuffles up again.

This is the Victorian church my father and mother
Were married in that Lenten day so long ago:
The courage, the confidence in life
The son has never found, yet had beginning
In this place. Now come back,
A public man, scarred with injuries,
Seared by experience, without illusion
Or any hope, dedicated to despair.

What hope in these tender trumperies
That move the heart, but not the hardened mind?
The moment comes, thurifer and acolytes

Around the priest, aloft the lights,
The church all silent for the Consecration.
Tears burn behind the unbelieving eyes,
Knowing too well no miracle is here
But dear mnemonic mummery.
A hush falls, the sanctus bell clangs out over
My cousin's grave , eager and gallant youth,
Over the roofs and down to the harbour.
At the Communion, one old sinner I used to know
In her more prosperous days returns to pew,
The haggard eyes not more suffused with tears
Than the known face that greets her after years
Looking up with a chaste and sad surprise.
The lights are out, the incense quenched,
The slim and stalwart thurifer
Back in his place in choir.
The moment of suspended time
Hung between now and eternity is over,
Tenderness floods into the unquiet heart
As the parish files out through the lych-gate
My parents entered some seventy years ago,
And scatters along the unrecoverable road.

The Faithful Unbeliever

I stand on the steps of St Peter's, Eaton Square,
Sparrows chirping under the tall colonnade,
The flowering cherry all in surpliced white,
Daffodils and bluebells this late reluctant May:
Rain and sun and wind, the scent of flowers,
The mingled beauty and sadness of the spring.
Within, here is the sanctuary where he served.
The verger says, 'He left before I came.
Several members of the congregation remember him.
He died this year, didn't he?'

This is where he served his first curacy,
A frisky young cleric straight from college,
Tall and boyish, full of pranks and fun.
Here's the pulpit where he preached his sermons
Beneath the hanging Master whom he served.
A secret stillness holds within this place,
Punctuated, not disturbed, by the traffic without.
Here's the font where he baptized, the scene
Of play-acting that was not all play-acting.
Spring flowers light up the sanctuary
With their gold. A flickering morning light
Passes over the altar where he often knelt,
Not at ease with himself, with difficulty
Attempting to follow in his Master's footsteps,
Not often achieving it, yet not wholly out.
Victorian mosaic and gilt, brass eagle and screen,
The angels look down upon the human scene:
Sunday by Sunday the choirboys and servers,
The rich dowagers of the Square, the streets around,
The School journey to his native Newquay,
The boy's Swimming Gala at St George's Baths,
The multifarious errands of the parish,
The life of good works, not unscathed by sin.

O, Anthony, how could it have come to this?
The fruitful life, the unsteady course, still
Yielding good, ended by its own will,
After what anguish of mind, what suffering,

Snuffed out like the sunlight flickering
On the altar, passing and repassing
This uncertain spring, perhaps a sign
Of recognition to one lingering in the church –
Darkness in the sanctuary as he withdraws –
The faithful unbeliever, remembering.

Cat-Fixation

I suffer from a malady
The sophisticated call
Cat-fixation.

Wherever I go I find
Those winning ways
Await me.

Agate eyes, shell-whorl ears,
Gestures of instant beauty
And insinuation.

Loving to lie on whom they love
In ravishing attitudes,
Or feed by hand.

Expressions equally beguiling,
Acting 'wicked' or playing 'good'
In alternation.

With tail in rhythm waving –
No princess greets more sedately
From whatever station.

How could I endure to be without –
After despairing humans –
This consolation?

The White Cat of Trenarren

He was a mighty hunter in his youth
At Polmear all day on the mound, on the pounce
For anything moving, rabbit or bird or mouse –
My cat and I grow old together.

After a day's hunting he'd come into the house
Delicate ears stuck all with fleas.
At Trenarren I've heard him sigh with pleasure
After a summer's day in the long-grown leas –
My cat and I grow old together.

Now we are too often apart, yet
Turning out of Central Park into the Plaza,
Or walking Michigan Avenue against the lake-wind,
I see a little white shade in the shrubbery
Of far-off Trenarren, never far from my mind –
My cat and I grow old together.

When I come home from too much travelling,
Cautiously he comes out of his lair to my call,
Receives me at first with a shy reproach
At long absence to him incomprehensible –
My cat and I grow old together.

Incapable of much or long resentment,
He scratches at my door to be let out
In early morning in the ash moonlight,
Or red dawn breaking through Mother Bond's spinney –
My cat and I grow old together.

No more frisking as of old,
Or chasing his shadow over the lawn,
But a dignified old person, tickling
His nose against twig or flower in the border,
Until evening falls and bed-time's in order,
Unable to keep eyes open any longer
He waits for me to carry him upstairs
To nestle all night snug at foot of bed –
My cat and I grow old together.

Careful of his licked and polished appearance,
Ears like shell-whorls pink and transparent,
White plume waving proudly over the paths,
Against a background of sea and blue hydrangeas –
  My cat and I grow old together.

Native Sky

St Mabyn church tower tops the world,
In the south the woods of Pencarrow,
Clouds dapple the valley to St Kew;
In the field, tractor and harrow.

The farmboy whistles as he goes
Making his furrows across;
A white gull follows his dark shadow;
We sit by the wayside cross.

From the steps five churches appear:
St Endellion peeps a pinnacle,
St Eval punctuates the west,
St Minver spires the hill.

Stockinged cattle crop the stubble;
Above, the barrow's edge;
Afternoon sun on the face of St Kew,
A pheasant calls in the hedge.

A signpost points to St Endellion,
Chapel Amble, Wadebridge;
The gulls rise soundless from the loam,
Toadflax glints on the ledge.

The sleeping farms lie all around,
And never shall you and I
Meet again this magic moment
Under our native sky.

Easter at St Enodoc

O Mably and Treverton and Guy,
Here at St Enodoc they lie
Together beneath the twisted spire,
Across from Stepper and Pentire:

There runs the blue crystalline sea
Beyond the open estuary,
Where breaks the line of surf and spray
On the Doom Bar of Padstow Bay.

Tamarisk shrouds the church around:
There's the quarry whence came the stone,
Many a headstone on its mound
Lit at night by the light from Trevone.

Here a seaman cast on shore,
Far from the home his footsteps trod,
Nameless, alone, in time of war:
'Unknown to us, but known to God.'

Easter has garnished the graves with flowers
Placed by many a friendly hand;
Tumulus clouds and late March showers
Threaten across the shadowed land.

Up the lane the poet lives,
Flowering currant at his door:
Inspiration receives, and gives,
From hill and valley, stream and shore.

Within the church the candles are lit,
Flicker upon the upturned faces,
Where the assembled parish sit
In their accustomed pews and places.

Spring flowers brighten sill and pew,
Put about by the faithful few;
From the west a transient gleam
Upon the figures rapt in dream:

The western window says, bright and clear,
'He is risen. He is not here.'
Scent of grass and Easter sun,
Service is over and day is done.

St Endellion

The little tower stands sturdy on the dead
Looking out to sea, to Kellan Head
And over Atlantic miles away to Lundy.
Here came the faithful forbears Sunday by Sunday
From farms of hereabouts, Trelights, Tresunger,
From the labour of their lives to stay their hunger
With hope of rest and peace: who now lie here
Beneath their headstones to tell us who they were
When they were alive. They do not cease to be
When the bells ring out over the land and sea
Calling us to church and festival,
Music and lights. Around us the prebendal
Houses, crouching from Atlantic wind,
Mottled and mossy from time out of mind,
Huddle like cattle on the distant moor
Southward to Brown Willy and Rowtor.

Through the summer hedgerow lanes we come
Over the hills and valleys from our home –
Honeysuckle, campion, August flowers,
Meadowsweet and ragwort to tell the hours,
Until time to enter, group by group;
We pass Roscarrock's holy-water stoup,
Genuflect to Endellion's elvan shrine,
Borne to burial here by eight white kine.
The congregation safely gathered in,
Subdued air of excitement, a friendly smile,
The faithful greet each other across the aisle –
While Nicholas Billing, a grey slate on the wall,
A white surround, looks down to bless us all,
And we are lost: the music has us in thrall,
Voices and violins make festival.
Time passes with the music's cadences,
The sense of ebb and flow of centuries ...
Night falls; and we come forth from the Requiem,
The crowding gravestones nod, Remember them.

Yarcombe Hill

On Yarcombe Hill the birds sing shrill
  While Geoffrey and I toil on our way;
The road winds steeply down to the bridge.
  And all is glad on a summer's day.

We look across the heave of the hill
  Where Sheafhayne manor secret lies:
Ransomed by Drake with Spanish gold
  Captured beneath Pacific skies;

Lived in still by the family's
  Descendant, a young Guards' officer,
Returned from the war to continue the line,
  Francis Drake's last, ultimate heir.

On Yarcombe Hill the wind blows cold
  Across the valley from Sheafhayne;
Down the path and in at the porch
  Alone I shelter from autumn rain.

The wind blusters around the church,
  The half-hour bursts upon the chime;
Within, I pace the aisle and mark
  The monuments of former time.

Near the altar I note the tablet
  To the young soldier's memory –
Already inscribed ten years ago:
  'He liveth in eternity.'

All around the saints stand still,
  St James with staff and scallop-shell,
St Peter with his key, St John,
  The Virgin in her tabernacle.

On Yarcombe Hill the snow lies thick
  Upon the silent winter slopes,
All down to where the River Yarty
  Dark under frozen surface sleeps.

Turning to go, behind me the gate
  Clangs above my muffled tread,
Awakes me, Geoffrey, from my dream:
  I cannot remember you are dead.

Marytavy

Marytavy, Marytavy,
  Blinking in the August sun,
We draw up at the churchyard gate
  After a Sunday morning run,

Up the valley from Tavistock,
  Skirting the edges of the Moor –
No one for church at Petertavy,
  Silent the bells and locked the door.

On we go around the gorge
  Over the narrow bridge we slow:
A couple of fishermen at the weir –
  This summer's drought the water's low.

And all around is spiritual drouth,
  Nonconformity in Devon
Dried up, the Methodist chapel shut:
  No one to go that way to Heaven.

And what shall we find at Marytavy?
  Apprehensively we search
Up the path and in at the porch –
  To find the parish all in church.

Six candles flare upon the altar,
  There all dressed in ferial green,
Out from the vestry pops the priest,
  Biretta and chasuble brightly seen;

Shuffling behind his acolytes two,
  Spectacles on the tip of his nose.
Under the roodscreen, into the chancel
  And up the altar steps he goes.

All three genuflect together,
  He takes the incense-boat in hand,
Gives the altar a thorough censing,
  While very reverently we stand;

And all the parish sings the Mass
  In plainchant to the manner born,
The *Gloria* first; it's all as if
  The Reformation had never been.

Here on the western slopes of Dartmoor
  The incense mingles with morning air:
Lost in thought, I lose my place,
  Look up, and see the priest is there,

Coming down the aisle, with flick of wrist
  Besprinkles the folk with holy water;
Unaccustomed, to my surprise,
  I suddenly receive a spatter.

Unexpectedly sanctified,
  Rather abashed, we beat a retreat;
The Mass goes on, but all around
  At Marytavy the air is sweet.

Winter in Stratford Church

The winter wind rattles in roof and rafter,
Yet all the townsfolk are in church – needs must.
The morning's milk came frozen home in pail.
A flurry of snow dusts the churchyard path
By the charnel house where he saw his little boy:
'I am afraid, and yet I'll venture it.'
The choir where canons of the College prayed
Is empty now, boarded up, derelict.
Hear the rain and wind beat dark December,
Loosen the leads, worry the quarried panes
Where once glowed saints in all their coloured glory,
Brasses ripped up, slave to mortal rage.
Late-comers arrive, shuffle along to pew,
Huddle together to keep warm in their own steam
That mingles with smoke of brazier at the back,
Spiralling up into the tower by the font,
Where he and all the family were christened.
Now they are gathered up in front, below
The pulpit where coughing drowns the parson's saw.

Suddenly a word is dropped into that well
Of the imagination, the listening ear:
'Therefore hath he mercy on whom he will
Have mercy, and whom he will he hardeneth.'
The ears that hear everything that people say,
Shut out the noises of the congregation,
While thoughts stir behind the secret forehead.
'On my frailties why are frailer spies,
Which in their wills think bad what I think good?
No: I am that I am.'

   The homely wife
Sits unstirred, unnoticing beside him,
Or how much does she know or guess, who keeps
Silence, never uttering a word?
Remorse of conscience for what cannot now be helped
Enters crevices, thoughts cohere
While eyes wander around the white-washed walls
That yet not obliterate the Risen Lord

In judgment, the Doom looking on the scene,
The good and bad in everyone, the true
And seeming, the ineradicable fault
In nature. Words from around the Figure
Now but a shadowy outline on the Cross:
'Why, all the souls that were, were forfeit once
And he that might the vantage best have took
Found out the remedy. How would you be
If He, which is the top of Judgment, should
But judge you as you are. O, think on that!'

Lines for William Shakespeare

Reading in a book I came upon the words
In some dull prose,'Thou hast nor youth nor age
But, as it were, an after-dinner's sleep
Dreaming on both.' The words leaped from the page:
Surprised, I suddenly found myself in tears.
There was that voice, the very rhythm and accent,
Simple, familiar, yet unmistakable,
Reaching across the yet unnumbered years,
The centuries, to touch the waiting heart.
And now again he says, 'There's no art
To find the mind's construction in the face.'
But in the magical mastery of phrase
That reaches the hidden crevices of guilt,
Remorse for what is irremediable,
That strips away pretence, hypocrisy,
The blindness to what we've done, and bares the wound.
One can hardly bear to look – a scene in a play
No longer, but the truth of life itself:
The bitter words of Hamlet to his love,
Because he loves, but believes he is betrayed;
Macbeth's wife, walking in her sleep,
Washing her hands, but blood will not away.
Leontes looks upon the ruin of his life,
Reconciled, forgiveness at the last.
Lear to the daughter he had disowned,
'Your sisters have, as I do remember, done
Me wrong. You have some cause; they have not.'
To which Cordelia: 'No cause, no cause.'
Such words sear the heart, and search the brain.
There never has been anyone like him.

Letter to Larkin

Dear Philip, I'm coming to my end too,
A decade and more older than you,
And your view of life just isn't true.
You made poetry out of sheer misery,
Out of the eldering man yourself,
Getting up in the night to piss
Half-drunk, after the hopelessness
Of the day's workload – the Toad.
Why not a day off, take the road
Out of the confines of Hull, your Hell,
To drink the beauty of landscape, sun on sea?
Instead of watching dawn creep up the curtain
I throw open the window and face sunrise,
Drink at the orange flame of the skies
Above the still and waiting ice-blue bay.
A moment later the light suffuses
Honey through the trees' meshed filigree,
And it is day ...
Life isn't all misery
When out of it comes poetry.

Te lucis ante terminum

Reading high up in my New York room,
My eye falls on the words in Dante,
Te lucis ante:
The years fall away, and I hear
The voices of the youths we were
Lifted up towards the end of day
In that same hymn in lighted choir
At Oxford; I sense the spirit we put in
The ancient words for compline
In unison, gallant and surpliced,
Under the vigilant eye of bird-like Dean
And gathered dons – Julian, Tom and I.
Julian, who was to face a charge of treason,
Tom, mathematical and pious, against reason
Would submit to medieval discipline,
And I remain, dedicated to memory.
The day over, full of eager activity,
Night closing down on cloister and hall,
Light reflected in plashing Mercury –
I hear our vanished voices in the room,
Te lucis ante terminum,
And recognise from far away
The closing of our day.

All Souls Day

Justorum animae in manu dei sunt.
Brightly, warmly descends the autumn sun
On the morning chapel, and it is All Souls day.
The shadow of a bird passes up the painted
Glass, even as our lives in time will pass –
Colours on reredos and rows of the dead,
Amethyst and saffron, rose, blue, green.
Here they are gathered in mind who all are gone.

The ancient Warden reads the Founder's prayer,
Silvery hair, grey eyes, clean-shaven face,
His 'Pembers' a tuft of hair on each suave cheek.
Sermon by Henson, of beetling eyebrows
And clacking teeth, hissing across to Lang
How his predecessor at Durham, 'Analogy' Butler,
Had refused the primacy for 'he would not be
A pillar of a declining Church': on me
Not lost, for he wanted the see of York.
Old Oman whom Henson reproved for being late,
'Not only for the General Confession but
The Absolution you most stand in need of.'

Quavering-voiced, sharp-tongued Johnson, chaplain
And hunting parson, who closed discussion with
'Never ask for anything, never refuse anything,
And never resign anything' – wrestling with Morrah's
Soul, bent on going over to Rome:
Whose panegyric Reggie Harris preached
Improbably in Westminster Cathedral.
Reggie moves out, birdlike, head on one side:
I think of his jokes,
Handel, 'the great master of the common chord'.
Carcassonne, 'Violé par Le Duc.'

They all move up in seniority
To make their offering at the altar.
Robertson, sharp of nose and kind of heart,
Loquacity his only vice. And now
Comes Geoffrey Dawson of the *Times,*

Of fatal influence on foreign policy,
With his friend the 'Prophet' Curtis, who had
A message for the world, but lost his way.
Another wounded by loss in a later war.

Behold Spencer Wilkinson in spats
Shuffling with myopic gait up the steps,
Who'd have one think he had enjoyed the favours
Of Sarah Bernhardt: soft of heart:
A military man, marsh-mallow within.
McGregor, muttering to himself, having
Been blown up on the Menin Road –
That earlier war,
Began the ruin of the age in which we live.

Woodward served in Salonica; see him
With sceptical smile and clerical trail,
Approach the communion rail.
Bridges, of frosty eye and intellect,
Secrets of state well down 'in the deep, deep freeze'.

Pares, at whose election the Warden dreamed
Primus inter pares:
On whose beloved head cruel fate
Fell, unable to move muscle or limb.
Summer afternoons we'd sit beneath
The whitebeam's canopy and watch the sky
Wheeling over battlement and spire,
While time ate up the precious hour.

They all served Church or State in their day
Who now are here, shrouded in surplices
As once they were, and now are ghosts, alive
Only in the dedicated mind.
November sunlight flickers across the aisle,
Falls upon stall and altar, whereon
The candles shed their flame, and it is written:
The souls of the just are in the hand of God.

Trafalgar Square

Behold this quarry of human history,
Or, rather, of an empire at an end.
Nelson aloft against October cloud and sky,
Beneath, the monuments of the nation's past,
Disjecta membra of a happier time.
Here is Napier, 'erected by public subscription,
The most numerous of them being private soldiers';
Here Havelock, of the Indian Mutiny,
Commanding Oude Irregulars, Bengal Engineers,
Madras Fusiliers and Highland Foot.
The brightly striped and saaried Indian girls
Are being photographed beneath the hero:
All the flotsam and jetsam from the once
Gorgeous East, turbaned and camera-hung.

Tread softly, for you tread on my dreams,
Or on the congregated pigeons sober
As in church; here and there one flies up
On a fancier's shoulder, not however on mine.
The present holds no honour for me, only
The dream of the past, this graveyard of monuments,
Fossils of a more glorious, more amusing
Clime. The absurd Regent prances on horse,
The columns of his vanished Carlton House
For background, looks vacantly at Nelson.
Did this Regent of fantasy think that he
Was at Trafalgar? What would Nelson reply?
Turn a blind eye to the wheeling sky?

St Martin's steeple chimes a quarter to four:
A pallid sun peeps out to light the page,
The moving finger of time that writes, the man
Himself but a shadow column of his age.
Look down Whitehall, to the vista of Big Ben
And the former Mother of Parliaments: no future
There. Look down the once imperial way,
As the melancholy fated king looks down,
Contemplates his own last tragic day.

October sun runs up the fluted column,
And it is Trafalgar Day. Nelson is lost,
Far removed from the reeling world below:
A world in dissolution and decay,
The demos at ease, and everywhere out of control.

Intimations of Mortality

I am haunted by the idea of this poem,
Intimations of Mortality –
Haunted by visions of what I once did see
From early childhood, years of innocence,
Moments when the envelope of experience
Was broken to reveal images
To remain constants in my life and heart –
Mirrors to reflect eternity?
I do not know: only the images
Remain, inhabit a secret world unchanged.
The years do not blemish them, neither decay
Nor any stain deface their purity.

Before the poor cottage of tumbled thatch
Stood a group of straggling apple-trees,
The child beneath looked up through criss-cross branches
To catch a glimpse of blue sky unseen
Before – and saw a vision of the Civil War:
No angels ascending and descending like Jacob's
But the feeling he had seen it all before,
The strange sensation that he had been there –
But where? – as if it were a shaft into
The secret heart of the universe withheld,
Withdrawn – and now revealed unto a child.
That moment saw his first awareness flower
And, like a flower, the mystery closed upon
The blue depths of unfathomable sky.

But earlier still, so early he could never
Be sure whether experience or dream,
He stood in the summer dawn upon the shore
Of long Crinnis beach, when the seines were drawn
And, behold, a miraculous draught of fishes,
A myriad scales shone silver in the sun;
The whole inner bay shimmered and spun
With movement, as if the sea itself were alive,
The drawn fish thronging the golden sand.
The child was there with the men and fisherfolk:
It was no dream, the experience was real.

As years passed, the memory was blurred –
He knew no longer what the vision meant.
Was it Crinnis or the Sea of Galilee
Where it happened, and who were the men among whom
He was a stranger, unrecognised and alone?

A growing boy, a more familiar scene:
Leading his donkey in the dark before dawn
Under a firmament of stars – to be shod
At the smithy before the day's work began.
Suddenly he was aware as never before
Of the granite cottages asleep, the starry
Silence and the spread canopy of lights
That spanned the village, the darkness visible,
And all things were clear as they shall be made clear
At the latter day. For that moment time stood still.
Yet the memory of that moment lasted
All his life, into unquesting age.

Then, coming home from church, breasting the hill,
Breathing the keener air from Carclaze downs,
Turning he saw the harvest moon would fill
The bowl of the bay, brimming with luminous gold.
Perfection of the scene would stir the sense
Strangely with unease – wherefore, and why?
He stood at the gate, the threshold of mystery,
A return of the self upon the self, a voyage
Into the bidding night upon seas strange
Yet familiar, as if visited before:
Enticed, yet always voyaging alone.

Other such moments have accompanied him
Upon the journey of years, the ladder of life:
War-time evensong when the summer sun
Transfigured the western window of the church
To coloured glory and the Apostles shone;
While down below service of intercession
For men's lives went on. We prayed in vain.
The revelation was in the glow of light,
The sense of a world halted and transformed.

Nor less in later life, an eldering man
Was he the visionary consolation
Denied. In the toil and moil of daily work,
All unbidden, at the corner of the eye
Would come the visitation to announce
Time standing still: the copper-beech there
For ever, the frozen eagle with spread wings
Eternally poised for flight into the unknown,
The invitation of the Italian sky.

What to make of it? I cannot say.
Here and now we cannot know. I know
Only that these moments have sustained me,
Given food to the spirit, nourished mind
And imagination in the forlorn spaces,
Shafts of light into the heart of things
Though the mystery remain immutable.

The Veil

The finger of God, the finger of God –
Is he reaching out to me, I wonder?
I cannot tell. I only know
I am unworthy
I have not yet achieved
Transparency
To myself – I cannot see
My way – I am blind
I can only feel
What is behind
The veil.

11/93
5/95